Give
the Gift
of Healing

Give the Gift of Healing

A Concise Guide to
Spiritual Healing

ROSEMARY ALTEA

EAGLE BROOK

WILLIAM MORROW AND COMPANY, INC.
New York

Published by Eagle Brook
An Imprint of William Morrow and Company Inc.
1350 Avenue of the Americas, New York, N.Y. 10019

Library of Congress Cataloging-in-Publication Data

Altea, Rosemary.
    Give the gift of healing : a concise guide to spiritual healing /
    by Rosemary Altea.
        p.   cm.
    ISBN 0-688-15511-1
    1. Healing—Religious aspects.   I. Title.
    BL65.M4A58   1997
    615.8'52—dc21   97–11531
                                                     CIP

Printed in the United States of America

First Edition

1   2   3   4   5   6   7   8   9   10

BOOK DESIGN BY GIORGETTA BELL MCREE

To God—my heavenly father.

To Christ—my inspiration and my light.

To Grey Eagle—my teacher and my friend.

Knowing all of my life, my earthly life, that if I stray from my path, have strayed from my path, that my Father God will lovingly lead me back.

Knowing, since I have known Christ, which is all but two years of my earthly life, that even though I strive to hear him, to be as he would wish me to be, that I fail time and time again, still he leadeth me beside still waters.

Knowing Grey Eagle, gratefully accepting my role as his student, as poor a student as he perhaps will ever have, with my human faults and failings, still he loves me, still he trusts me to be a voice for the spirit world.

Truly, I am blessed . . . so very blessed.

And to my child . . . for she is truly my own blessed gift of healing. She smiles that smile meant only for me, and I am bathed in light.

Acknowledgments

From the beginning of my time as a teacher of spiritual healing I have had many students. Many have left, gone on to walk a different path, each one leaving behind a little of themselves. Each, hopefully, taking a little from me. For that which they gave to me I would like to say thank you.

Then there are those who have stayed. Dedicating their lives to healing. Striving to live each day all that they have learned, often failing as we all do, even so, never giving up the struggle. These are the people I wish to acknowledge here.

My team.

Without them there would be no healing organization.

Without them there would, over the years, have been thousands of people, patients of the Rosemary Altea Association of Healers (RAAH), sick and often desperate people, less fortunate than they were. People who were touched in a very special way.

Without them my life would be less than it has been, would have been emptier.

My team.

I am their teacher.

I have high standards and expectations.

My standards have been met.

My expectations have been surpassed.

They are truly dedicated, and from my heart, and with all of my heart, I thank them.

My team.

Their place is here beside me, as it was when the healing tape *Give the Gift of Healing* was created.

This small band of healers, headed by our chairman, Peter Boulton, "give the gift of healing" every day. All I can give in return is the gift of love.

Contents

Question: Grey Eagle, would you please explain how spiritual healing works and how we would know if we are capable of giving healing?

Answer: I am Grey Eagle. I am Shaman.

Within my heart lies the power to heal. I have great power... great strength, and for this, I am seen as a great man... a wise and knowing entity.

But I will tell you, from my heart, that I have no more or less than each of you. For within each of you is the ability to heal ... to heal not only your own selves but to give healing to others also.

Again, by using your thought process and creating thought pattern... and using the power which you own... and by joining with that universal force... that God force which is good and true... the power to heal is yours... for everyone... for every living being.

For some it may be greater than for others, but even as a child falls and grazes its knee, a mother will pick up this child and, placing her hand on the child's knee, rub it better. She gives healing to the child... an unconscious thing. For somewhere within...deep within her...her soul will tell her that this she can do.

Within the universe there are no limits.

And with right thought and with right heart, each human soul has the power to create healing energy and to use that healing energy for his or for her own benefit or for the benefit of others.

And it is for the individual...for each soul...to decide how and when, and how is best to use this energy.

And it is only for me to tell you that you own the power. And, once again, I say this to you.

Introduction

Give *the Gift of Healing* is a concise guide, an introduction to my role as a healer. As I came to the end of my writing, my fingers itched. There was a need in me to write more. For the subject of healing is of great interest to me, and I have a vast experience, not only as a healer, but as a teacher of the healing arts. There is within me a well, a deep, deep well, rich with information, healing stories, and wise teachings.

Here in this small book is just a taste of things to come. For my fingers, my mind, my heart, are itching to write more, a fuller book . . . and soon, very soon, I will start to work on this.

In the meantime, let me introduce myself. I have been a healer for more than fifteen years.

But wait, that isn't quite true. For I have been a healer for all of my life, even before my life here on this earth. As we all have been, as we all are.

So let me begin again.

I have been a *practicing* healer for more than fifteen years. Working as a teacher, working with the sick and dying, learning more than I teach, receiving more than I give.

I "give the gift of healing," and in giving, I have received, more than tenfold.

Again, I "give the gift of healing," and it is given back to me again and again.

This is what healing is. Giving out, and receiving, giving out, and receiving, giving out, and receiving. Giving love. Gaining love. And first, before giving to anyone else, we must learn to give to ourselves.

That is in part what this book is about. For until we have learned and experienced the art of giving to ourselves, how do we know how much there is of us to give to others?

This, then, is the first rule for all healers. To learn that it is OK to be a little selfish with oneself. To understand that it is right that we should love ourselves, that we can indulge ourselves a little. To know that it is necessary for our health and well-being.

As a healer, and having seen many healers at work over the years, I know the importance of giving to myself.

I owe it to my patients to stay healthy. I owe it to my friends to remain well. I owe it to my daughter.

And of course, I owe it to myself. After all, what use would I be to anyone if I neglected me?

And so, even as I write this book, I will indulge myself. When I describe the colors and use of color in healing, even as I write, I will visualize those colors, I will absorb their energy, and as I write, I will give to myself. I will GIVE THE GIFT OF HEALING.

Let us begin. Let us begin with the words that can be heard on my first healing tape, *Give the Gift of Healing*. You do not have to listen to the tape to grasp the ideas it expresses, but you can play it as you read along if you like. Yes, I think this is a good place to begin.

Give
the Gift
of Healing

Your Journey Toward Healing

PREPARING THE JOURNEY

Hello, my name is Rosemary Altea, and I am a medium and a healer. Together with my guide, Grey Eagle, and through his inspiration, I have founded and helped to run the RAAH, the Rosemary Altea Association of Healers, a healing association that has membership throughout the world.

Many mediums and healers have spirit guides, and I am no exception. A few years ago, when I first came into this work and heard talk of spirit guides, my attitude was very dismissive. I simply could not comprehend that such beings not only existed, but could become involved with ordinary beings on this earth plane in an earthly and down-to-earth way.

I have since been proved wrong. My closed-minded

view has now broadened, and I accept that with my limited vision, being mere mortal, I can only comprehend a mere fraction of what can and does exist on a universal level.

Grey Eagle is a highly evolved spirit being who spent his time of learning on this earth plane as an American Indian, an Apache. He is not only my guide, my teacher, and my mentor but also my best friend. He helps me to discover wisdom through his words and strength through his teaching. We walk hand in hand to bring to this tortured world a ray of hope, a ray of light, and a ray of understanding. We believe that all endings, even the ultimate ending, which is death, bring new beginnings and new life. We unite in harmony and truth, wishing to share with people all over the world the greatest of God's gifts, which is love. We learn that even through our pain, our suffering, and our sorrows, there is always a spark of light remaining to show the way for our tomorrows.

Healing is first and foremost a healing of the inner self, that part which some may call the spiritual self. We try, through meditation and by creating healing energies, to bring about a calm and a peace to that spiritual self. Healers believe in the power of thought and in the use of mind energy. It is important, then, to remember the power of thought and to explore its potential. Thought is so potent that it materializes itself through the ether so then, what we think, we become.

How important, then, is it that we need to control our thought process, to remember that the mind controls the body? We can use the creative power of thought, harness it and put it to work, to work for us. Thoughts are living things, and so it is with creative and with constructive thought that the healing energy that is within us can be developed. Combine this energy with the divine healing energy, which comes from God, which some may call universal energy, and you have at your disposal a massive source of healing energy. Through the use of this energy we will learn to use the knowledge that we gain from this exploration and to discover a new depth, a new dimension, not only of our own selves but of the powerful energy that is universal and available to us all.

We will discover the importance of breathing and of breathing in, using the solar chakra, one of the seven main energy points of the body, which seats itself near to the solar plexus. All of us at some time in our lives have experienced the use of this energy center. Most of us would understand butterflies in the stomach, a churning or sick feeling when we are tense or nervous. It is that area which pinpoints this center of energy. Encouraging this energy center to open and to do its work will enable us not only to absorb external or universal energy but it also enables us to create and to be constructive with our own inner energy. And so we breathe in, using this energy center, drawing in energy through our solar plexus, visualizing the solar chakra as a vortex taking in energy, creating more energy.

The word "chakra" is a Hindu word meaning spinning wheel. And so we visualize around the area of the solar plexus a small round wheel spinning slowly at first, and gently acting as a vortex, it gathers in and helps us to absorb that wonderful healing energy, so full of vitality, so full of life, and so positive.

I feel that it is important to mention the very great significance to our lives of our emotions. Love, hate, frustration, longings, yearnings, hope, joyfulness, despair. All of our emotions, feelings, are pure energy, and we use them knowingly or unknowingly, either constructively or destructively, positively or negatively.

The most powerful of our emotions is love. Love can be seen as passion or as caring. It can be seen as gentleness or as kindness. Love in whatever form stirs feelings, creates energy. True loving is unselfish and creates the need to give. The art of giving not only to others but also to our own selves is in understanding the need to receive.

Many of my patients are people who have either forgotten or who have brushed aside their own need to receive. People who have been so concerned with the need to work, with the need to provide in a material sense for their families, with the needs of their children, their parents, their friends. Not only have they ignored their own health, but more, they have not even considered their own need for inner peace. That peace which will only come by creating a state of mind and body that brings about spiritual harmony. It is my hope that this information will help you on your way to achieving just such a state of being.

As a spiritual healer I use color energy, healing energy, not only with all of my patients but with all of my students as well. It is helpful therefore to have some sort of guide to the meaning and type of energy that each color is. So I will mention briefly some of the colors that I might use, in the hope that this will help you with your creative thought process (see page 29 for a fuller discussion). Please remember that you should use this information as a guide only. I am not saying that each color has a certain meaning but merely that the use of certain colors in certain ways can be beneficial. It will be up to you whether or not this proves to be the case.

✳

We begin with the color blue.

Blue is the universal healing color and to my knowledge is used by all spiritual healers in their work.

*

Green. The use of the color green aids in harmony and unity. Green is used as the color that denotes peace.

*

Red. This color is stimulating and brings life-giving rays of power. As a teacher I advise my students to use this color sparingly and with gentleness.

*

Rose pink. A gentle color, bringing love and warm affection. This color is most often used in relation to matters of the heart and emotions.

*

Mauve. The enhancement of this color can bring about aid to discovering wisdom and the desire to understand the mind.

*

Purple. This is a color we see a great deal of in our churches and places of worship; therefore we associate the color purple with religious bodies. For the purpose of healing we can, if we so wish, use this color to encourage strength, growth, and power.

*

Gold. The color gold connotes wisdom, joy, hope, laughter, and happiness. This is a color of great strength and opportunities.

*

Silver. This color, the color of silver, in all its beauty, brings spiritual love.

✳

These colors that I have mentioned are only a few of the colors that a healer might use in his or her work. Through visualization and energy creation we can, with time, patience, and lots of practice, create a state of mind and being that is full of vibrant, brilliant color, full of life. We can, with perseverance, create beautiful, positive, and constructive healing energy. And in so doing, we discover a way to create peace and harmony and light, the essence of being and of being whole.

Many of my patients, people who are ill, their bodies racked with pain and suffering, come to me desperate for a cure, desperate for help to ease the pain. One such patient, Wendy, was the inspiration for the audiotape *Give the Gift of Healing.* Her body was racked with pain and suffering, her mind in a state of torment. She is a beautiful lady who is now in the spirit world. Her need, her need for the light, her need to see the blue light of healing, not only to see it but to feel it, for it to surround her in order that she should begin to feel whole again, was a major inspiration to me and gave me the strength and the courage to make the tape for her and for the many people like her. Throughout the tape I feel Wendy's love with me. She was helped on her journey.

Now we begin a journey, the journey of the self toward the self. Creating a state of inner peace and spiritual harmony. Thus creating a state of self-healing. We will take the light of love and sprinkle it all around, and within its heart you will be found. Take the light of hope from us to you and within its heart some healing love for you. Take our strength; we give it you. Our healing rays go out to you.

THE JOURNEY BEGINS: A SELF–HEALING EXERCISE

I would like you now to find a comfortable chair to sit in, or a bed to lie on. Make yourself as comfortable as possible, and we will begin. Close your eyes, and allow your mind to absorb the music of your choice. Breathe in deeply but gently, using your solar plexus, and bring to mind, if you can, the color blue.

You may visualize a blue sky, a warm and inviting Mediterranean Sea, or just lots and lots of blue ribbons floating gently on a cool breeze. Breathe in gently, and let the music work to help you to relax. Again breathe in deeply but gently, using your solar plexus, and visualize the color blue. Now, slowly and carefully, begin to visualize the color green. And then, as you begin to create your picture, bring to it the color gold and the color pink. Make your picture a beautiful one, a rainbow of color, yours alone for you to look at and to become part of. Your picture, a picture of healing.

You have created a rainbow of color. Now allow this rainbow of color to wash over your body. Cleansing, bringing light, making you whole. The rainbow of color becomes a waterfall, and as you stand beneath it, its waters wash over you. Let the water wash away the hurt and pains that illness creates.

You become part of that waterfall. The waterfall joins the stream, the stream of life. And in its strength it gives to us new life, new hope, and renewed strength. Take the light of love, and sprinkle it all around, and within its heart you will be found. Take the light of hope from us to you and within its heart some healing love for you. Take our strength; we give it you. Our healing rays go out to you.

Now I would like you to visualize me. I am standing by the side of you; my hands, cool, strong, reassuring, I place upon your head. Feel my strength; feel the energy, that healing energy which comes from that divine source. Use it; it's yours to use. Breathe in gently; feel my fingers caressing your forehead. Blend your energy with mine, and together we will create a powerful and positive source of healing. Let it work; let it happen. Relax and feel the joy of just being; be you.

Ask and it shall be given unto you. We ask for healing and for divine love.

The cold, clear strength in the flow of the stream, within it you become what you seem. As the cold, clear stream flows through, you enter it and become you. Its water's icy fingers touch your face, and like cobwebs, all your thoughts become as lace. You place yourself within its heart; you become the stream and not apart. It cleanses you; the light is clear; its waters wash away your fear. Like music, let it flow through you. Allow your thoughts to be clear and true. Your meditation does the spirit show; your life does as the spirit, as the stream, flow.

A paradise of color fills the stream, a ray of light, a golden beam. You swim amidst the rainbow hue, the greens, the gold, the shades of blue. The sun burns bright, a brilliant sun, shines on the water, a new day begun. The stream and you, and you the stream, become that light, that golden beam. Become those colors, gold, green, and blue, become pure power through and through. And gentleness, like drops of rain, begins to wash away the pain. And as the water flows its way, your heart does know your spirit, here to stay. Your meditation does the spirit show; your life does as the spirit, as the stream, flow.

I'm still here, still by your side, giving healing, giving love.

And once again, the cold, clear strength in the flow of the stream, within it you become what you seem. As the cold, clear stream flows through, you enter it and become you. Its water's icy fingers touch your face, and like cobwebs, all your thoughts become as lace. You place yourself within its heart. You become the stream and not apart. It cleanses you; the light is clear. Its waters wash away your fear. Like music, let it flow through you, allow your thoughts to be clear and true. Your meditation does the spirit show. Your life does as the spirit, as the stream, flow.

A paradise of color fills the stream, a ray of light, a golden beam. You swim amidst the rainbow hue, the greens, the gold, the shades of blue. The sun burns bright, a brilliant sun, shines on the water, a new day begun. The stream and you, and you the stream, become that light, that golden beam.

The stream and you, and you the stream, become that light, that golden beam. Become those colors, gold, green, and blue, become pure power through and through.

And gentleness, like drops of rain, begins to wash away your pain. And as the water flows its way, your heart does know your spirit, here to stay. Your meditation does the spirit show; your life does as the spirit, as the stream, flow.

Take the light of love, and sprinkle it all around,

and within its heart you will be found. Take the light of hope from us to you and within its heart some healing love for you. Take our strength; we give it you. Our healing rays go out to you.

And together Grey Eagle and I will send to you our love.

Commonly Asked Questions About Spiritual Healing

Before I address some commonly asked questions about healing, I'd like to begin by explaining how members of the Rosemary Altea Association of Healers perceive the healing art. I, as the founder and teacher of this group, would like to share with you my thoughts and feelings about spiritual healing.

To do this, first I must explain that every living thing has an aura. Our aura, or energy field, surrounds us, extending above and beyond the skin by several feet. This energy field can be photographed, using a special camera developed by a Russian couple, Semyon and Valentino Kirlean, many years ago.

The soul too has its aura, its energy field. We refer to this energy as the spirit, the light that surrounds and gives light to the soul.

When we become physically sick, our ill health is mirrored in our aura, affects our aura, often affects our spirit. When the soul becomes needy, this too reflects in the soul's aura, our spirit, which will often dim. The light will become less bright, and the soul will struggle in the dark.

When I or my students give healing, first we ask for God's help, for His energy and His light. We ask that this energy be given first to the spirit, so that the soul's aura can become brighter and give more light to the soul. When this happens, a great healing will take place, and when the soul absorbs that healing energy, and when the soul finds that peace and enlightenment it so needs, then, often, a physical healing will take place.

So a spiritual healer will look first to give healing to the spirit, the light of the soul, not, as many suppose, to the cancer, to the arthritis, to the migraine, but first to the spirit.

Often, as the spirit absorbs its healing and responds well, the effects of healing will go beyond the soul, beyond the spirit, and will affect the physical body, create a physical "cure."

After the healer has given to the spirit, then it is time to work on the physical, to give healing energy to the tumor, to the broken bones, to the depression, or to whatever physical ailment there is. Further in the book I explain more about this and show you how you can do this for yourself.

Question: Rosemary, can you give a very simple definition of spiritual healing?

Answer: Healing is quite simply a harmonizing of the spirit, mind, and body.

Question: How does a healer help create that harmony?

Answer: A skilled healer has developed the art of "tuning in" to that higher source of power, of healing energy, that energy which I believe comes from God. He or she will be able to draw on that "God energy," to tap into the God source, and, with God's help, be able to direct that healing energy to the "patient."

Question: What steps does the healer take?

Answer: The healer will sit with his or her patient
               or, if that is not possible, visualize the pa-
               tient, and the patient's problem. He or she
               will send out to God, to the universe, a
               prayer, a request for energy, so that healing
               might take place. Always, when a healer
               does this, his or her priority is for the
               spirit, for the spirit of his or her patient.
               For a healer understands that the need for
               light, the need for healing, for growth, is
               the soul's need. I believe that the needs of
               the soul must be met first. If the soul can
               receive light, healing, love, then the physi-
               cal and emotional needs of the patient will
               respond, creating harmony, uniting the
               whole, and healing takes place.

Question: What is the laying on of hands?

Answer: Christ, one of the greatest of all healers,
               gave healing by placing his hands on his

patient. There are so many examples of this in the New Testament, and many modern-day healers try to follow Christ's example.

To "lay" your hands on someone, to touch, with love, with compassion, to reach out, to hold, to give, to pass on your energy, to be a channel for divine energy. To take the hand of someone in need of healing, to take that hand gently and with a wish that healing will find its way to that person, this is what the "laying on of hands" really means.

Question: Does healing always work?

Answer: I am so often asked this question, and my answer is immediate. I believe that healing works 100 percent of the time. This is a great claim, and how can it be? When I make this claim, I am aware that I must make my answer as clear as I can. I remember only too well how long it took for me to understand.

Each and every day every one of us has the ability to give healing, for healing is simply the act of one soul giving love to another soul. When the healer and the patient connect, for no matter how brief a moment that may be, the healer calls on his higher self, calls to his spirit, to his soul. The soul hears all, sees all, and responding to the call, the soul's heartbeat grows stronger.

The patient may or may not be aware that he or she is soul. The patient may be sleeping. But the soul never sleeps, and the soul of the patient will also hear the call of the healer, will also respond. And the soul of the patient, responding to the call, will grow stronger. And the heartbeat of the soul, as it grows stronger, will, in turn, give energy, healing energy, to the spirit.

For the call of the healer is the call of love.

And love is the name we give to the purest and most wonderful of all things . . . light.

Question: Can spiritual healing bring about a miracle?

Answer: So many people come to our healing organization hoping for a miracle. The miracle that will cure their cancer, enable the cripple to walk, the deaf to hear, the blind to see. And always, as a healer, whatever I feel my patient's prognosis to be, I ask for the miracle. As an old man, a healer of many years, once said to me, "There's no harm in asking. After all, if you don't ask, you may not get." So I ask for the miracle, and sometimes God grants my request.

However, there is always a miracle of some kind. Though to human eyes and human hearts this miracle may seem less than it is. Less dramatic than the physical cure, less exciting, less noticeable, less meaningful perhaps. But to God, to the eyes and hearts of the spirit world, to the universe, this is the real miracle, the miracle that stays with us, long after the physical body has wasted and died. This miracle is the enlightenment of the spirit. Light, pure healing light, which brings peace and harmony to the patient, which brings growth to the soul.

Question: Rosemary, is there a difference between a miracle and a cure?

Answer: According to Webster's dictionary, a cure is "spiritual care. Recovery or relief from disease." A miracle is: an extraordinary event manifesting a supernatural work of God.

I'm not sure I understand the difference or if indeed there is one. Life is full of small miracles, manifestations of God. In healing oneself, a miracle occurs. In giving healing to others, a miracle occurs. Perhaps a miracle is in the eye of the beholder, the one experiencing the miracle.

As far as I, the beholder, can see, a miracle is that which has God's hand to it. Divine, wonderful, a work of God, through which a "cure" may or may not be seen.

Question: What does the patient who dies get from healing?

Answer: As a healer I have sat at the bedside of many of my patients as they have faced death. It has been my privilege to have been with some at the point of death, to have held their hands as they have passed into the spirit world. And I have never seen healing fail. Always my patients have found peace, inner, deep, and meaningful peace, which has come through the power of God, the power of healing. I say this last with all humility and with grateful thanks to that higher power.

Question: What does the healer of a patient who dies get from healing?

Answer: To illustrate, I will tell you a story. The story of a healer whose husband was sick for many years.

Joan is my student, a full healer member of the RAAH, and we have worked together and been friends for more than twelve years.

More than four years ago her husband, Gerald, also my friend, had a massive heart attack. He survived, but over the following years he had many more. Surviving each one, he became weaker each time.

Apart from the healing he received regularly from my team, Gerald was given healing by Joan on a regular daily basis. She was now not only his wife of over forty years, she was his healer.

Often he would be rushed into hospital, and often we would hear the words "He won't pull through this time." But he was strong and stubborn, and he would simply fight his way back onto his feet.

Eventually his time came.

It was Christmas Day 1996. A few days earlier he had yet again been rushed into hospital.

Joan and I both knew, had been told by Grey Eagle, that it was his time to go.

He was sitting in his chair unable to lie down, hardly able to breathe.

Joan sat by his side, her hands on him, as usual, giving him healing.

They were alone. Just the two of them. He turned to her. "Joan, just put your hands on my throat. It hurts."

Joan reached forward, placed her healing hands gently on her beloved husband's throat.

He made a small sound, closed his eyes, and left.

And through her pain, and through her tears, the healer, the wife, the friend of so many years ... what does she say? How does she feel?

"I thank God that I was able to help him. That I was able to do something. That I wasn't helpless and could ease his pain." These words and more, much more, my friend has said to me in the weeks since her "patient" has died.

Question: Must healing be given in a particular place?

Answer: And I smile as I answer this question, knowing that many people are still unenlightened, still hold on to the old image of the dark room, the medium in a trance, those fabled words "Is there anybody there?" Healing can take place anywhere, anytime. In my second book, *Proud Spirit*™, I tell a story about a man, a patient, who had a healing session on a noisy, busy corner of a street in Hong Kong. Our healing

centers, rented rooms in community centers, are warm, light, and as comfortable as
we can make them. Healing can take place
in one's own home, in hospitals, wherever
the patient feels most comfortable. I have
even given healing on an airplane, not the
best place I agree, but anywhere the patient
is, God is there also.

Question: Do I need a healer? Is there a self-healing
exercise I can perform?

Answer: I am pleased to include this question, for
this is what this book is all about. Helping
us to "give" ourselves "the gift of healing."
Reading the section called "Your Journey
Toward Healing," on page I, will help
enormously (those of you who own the
healing tape will of course be able to build
on your visualization techniques).

In a further book, entitled *You Own the
Power!,* there are other exercises that will
also help.

Question: What about animals? Is it possible that our beloved pets can receive healing?

Answer: The answer is . . . definitely. As a healer and an animal lover I have many times been asked to give healing . . . to dogs and cats, birds, a tortoise once, horses, rabbits, and others. In *Proud Spirit*™ I tell the story of Karma, my own little boy, a King Charles Spaniel, and his brother, Jasper, and how at different times I gave them both healing. Animals are very receptive to healing, and I believe that we all have the ability to give healing, even if it is only in some small way. I will enlarge on this theory in my next book, *You Own the Power!*

Question: How does healing make us feel?

Answer: Calm, tranquil, rested. Some people experience a warming sensation, often, as if floating on a cloud. And there are some who feel no sensation at all, no heat, no cold, but later, relief from pain. Like any good medicine, if taken regularly, healing works, and the effects become more and more apparent.

Question: Is healing meant just for the sick?

Answer: Healing is for everyone, for every living thing, every plant, every tree, every insect ... yes, every insect, every animal, and of course, every human. Every living thing, regardless of faith, belief, way of life. Call it the power of God, the power of the universe, or the power of self; it doesn't matter; healing works for all.

So many of our patients come to me and my team of healers when all else has failed. When science has failed. But I believe that healing can act as a prevention against sickness. All it takes is just ten to fifteen minutes a day. "Give the gift of healing"; give it to yourself. It will help with the stresses and strains that, if ignored, can be the cause of sickness.

Healing is not just for the sick. It is, I believe, beneficial to us all.

Healing, for me personally? I see it as the power of God.

The power of God within.

And the power of the universe.

Which comes back to God.

And I thank God for the gift of healing, which he bestows on us all.

Question: Do you believe in traditional medicine?

Answer: As I explained in *The Eagle and the Rose*, I would not be alive today if it were not for the medical profession. I advise all of my patients to continue with or seek medical help. I believe doctors, healers, and patients should work together.

Question: What does color have to do with the healing process?

Answer: The answer to this question is: a great deal. In the next section of the book, "Healing Colors," you will see the role that color plays and the importance of color.

Healing Colors

Then God said, "Let there be light." And there was light. And God saw that the light was good.

In *The Eagle and the Rose* I quote the philosopher Teilhard de Chardin, who wrote, "We are spiritual beings having a human experience."

Spiritual beings. Beings of light. Each of us, each living thing, all that lives and breathes is light, and of God's light.

As we are taught in school, light, reflected through a prism breaks up into color.

My editor and friend Joann and I were having a conversation about this recently, and she told me how she was taught in school a way to remember these colors.

ROY.G.BIV.

Red. Orange. Yellow. Green. Blue. Indigo. Violet.

So, understanding that we are light, that our aura,

our energy field, is made up of colors, many shades and hues, we should not be surprised that spiritual healers use colors.

In fact the use of color by spiritual healers is universal. It comes with the understanding among healers that there are, within the universe, many different types of energy. The aura, the energy field that surrounds every living thing, is full of color: greens, reds, golds, etc. As our mood, our state of health, and well-being change, so too does our aura. Some colors become stronger, some lighter, some disappearing, only to reappear as our mood changes again. Our aura, made up of many colors, reflects who, how, and what we are.

This knowledge, a knowledge that all healers have, has been with us since time began. So it is not surprising that when giving healing, many healers will tap into that knowledge and use those different kinds of energy. Healers will visualize that energy as color, and use those colors.

As there are so many colors, shades, and hues, it would be impossible for me to describe them all and to show how they could be used in the healing process. But I thought it would be beneficial to take the eight colors mentioned earlier (see pages 5 to 7), and give a fuller explanation of the type of energy each color is and why a healer might use these colors.

I will begin with the color *BLUE...BLUE* is the

universal healing color. To my knowledge, this healing energy, seen as the color blue, is used by all healers, even those healers who do not work with auras and with other colors.

Why BLUE? you might ask. Why is BLUE the most prominent color? Why is the sky BLUE? Why is the grass green? The sun yellow? The stars silver? This is the nature of things universal, dictated by God, dictated by nature. This is simply the way it is. BLUE ... the universal healing color. As a healer I might suggest that my patient visualizes him/herself lying under a beautiful BLUE sky or wrapping him/herself in a soft BLUE blanket. This is a color that brings comfort and aids relaxation, a most important ingredient in the healing process.

Moving now to the color *GREEN*... The color that connotes peace. Certainly I would use this color to help stem anxiety and bring about calm. The color GREEN aids in harmonizing and uniting the soul, spirit, and body. How might I suggest my patient should visualize this color? Perhaps the best and most effective way that I have found is to imagine, visualize his or her feet slowly walking on soft, lush grass that has been warmed by the summer sun.

RED... The color RED seems to be the total opposite of that wonderful peacemaking green energy. A color of power, of vitality, of stimulation. I advise great care in the use of this color and will sprinkle it

oh, so gently and sparingly if my patient is suffering with depression or extreme tiredness. If you are
lacking energy, in need of a little vitality, then a
good exercise is to visualize a tiny speck or two of
RED, just a little splash, dancing in your aura. Don't
overdo it, though. You don't want to be dancing on
the ceiling!

One of my favorite colors now...*ROSE PINK*...
the color of warmth, of warm affection. In a world
where there is so much heartache, so much pain, this
energy is most needed, for it is the color that aids in
matters of the heart and emotions. It is said, and I
know this to be true, that a broken heart can be a
most painful thing, that it can even be a terminal illness.

There was a time, many years ago, when I was
twenty years old, seriously ill and in hospital, that I
met a woman. She too was seriously ill, had had many
tests, but no one could discover the reason for her
sickness. I was in bed, unable to move, and in great
pain. She—I have long since forgotten her name—
came to hold my hand. I remember her as quietly
spoken and gentle, and I remember her story. Her
husband had died suddenly and unexpectedly. They
had no children; there were just the two of them, a
devoted and loving couple. As she finished telling me
this, I remember her pausing, smiling a little, then

saying simply . . . "I have no reason to live without him."

The next day she was wheeled to the operating theater for an exploratory and minor operation. She never came out of the anesthetic.

I look back on that time, thinking, "If only I had known about healing then. If only I had understood how easy it is for us all to give a little healing, both to ourselves, and to others." Well, first I would have held this lady's hand. Then, having sent out a prayer to God, to the universe, for help, I would have visualized my patient, wrapped in a soft wool blanket the color of summer sky blue. I might then, knowing her sickness was of the heart and emotions, have visualized tiny threads of silk, the color of the most delicate and delicately perfumed soft-petaled rose, ROSE PINK. Gently, and with great care, painstaking and lovingly taking my time, I would have woven those perfect threads, in and out, back and forth, through the blanket. Weaving the energy up and down, around and around, building a protective and healing cocoon for my patient to lie within.

This method of healing—visualization—is very common and also very successful, for both the patient and the healer. It is a method I have encouraged my students to use, and also I would urge anyone wanting to try self-healing to use this approach.

Now to *MAUVE* . . . which is a deep and penetrating color. A color that can promote the desire to understand the mind. As a healer I would use the color MAUVE for any type of mental stress from depression on to the more serious diseases, such as schizophrenia.

Stress is also a sickness, as is confusion of the mind. I have many patients who come to me for help because they have a need, a desire, to climb out of the confused, stressed state that they are in and stay healthy. We can, any of us, I believe, do this only if we gain some understanding of who we are, how we think, and how we allow circumstances around us to affect our mental health. I would use the color MAUVE to help to improve any mental condition. As with all color, I would use it gently, lovingly.

A great exercise for "management under stress" is to spend just a few minutes every morning before work, and every evening after work, visualizing the color MAUVE. How you do it is up to the individual, but I personally might do it this way. My most indulgent time of the day is when I stand under the shower. It relaxes me, warms me, and if I feel mentally exhausted, I will visualize the water as it cascades over me, and I will visualize the water as a delicate and healing shade of MAUVE. I begin then, naturally, to unwind, to relax. I let my body, my mind, act like a sponge, and I throw myself wholeheartedly into the exercise of soaking up this powerful and positive energy. As I allow this process to take place, I can actually feel that energy penetrating right to the heart of me, healing my soul.

On to *PURPLE* . . . a color we see a great deal of in our churches and places of worship. This energy is powerful and can be used to promote strength and growth, both spiritually and emotionally. PURPLE is the color of encouragement. If I had a patient who was feeling, for whatever reason, helpless and hopeless, with no strength to fight his or her condition, I would reach out into that mass of universal God energy. Taking hold of that vital PURPLE, I might visualize it as many ribbons, soft, silky ribbons, dancing around and around, over and under, penetrating, becoming part of, my patient's aura. My aim would be to give my patient strength, not just physically but emotionally and spiritually too. If my patient can feel this strength as it enters him or her, then he or she might be encouraged. His or her feelings of helplessness and hopelessness might diminish a little. Growth takes place. Feeling this, he or she is encouraged, more in control, more powerful, more purposeful.

The sun, with all its power, all its warmth, deep and penetrating, revitalizing, speaks for the color *GOLD*. The energy of wisdom, joy, hope, laughter, and happiness. A color of great strength and opportunities. This is the color that shines out from most

of our children, from the energy, the aura, that surrounds them. In a school playground, a park, anywhere
we see groups of children, even on the dullest day, if
we could see energy, see auras, then we would see a
mass of GOLD, a live, shimmering, unrestrained mass
emanating from our youngsters. There is not one of
us who would not want this color, this energy. For
this is the color of life.

I remember the time I first discovered that I could
really see auras, individual energy fields. I was sitting
in my living room, reading a book and watching the
TV at the same time. Something caught my eye: something moving on the wall, in the corner of the room,
by the fireplace where I was seated. I swung my head
around to look, but at first I could see nothing. My
eyes moved back to the book, but again something
bright caught the corner of my eye. I looked again,
this time more closely. A tiny pinprick of light,
GOLD, it looked like a miniature torchlight, was
moving, oh, so slowly, up the wall. It took me a moment longer to notice the wood louse that seemed to
be trailing ever so slightly behind. My book forgotten,
I was intrigued. As I watched every now and then, the
light, which had appeared at first to be ahead of the
insect, would wash over the wood louse, just as a
searchlight might. It was only as the wood louse
turned and began to head in a different direction, the
light following, that I fully realized I was seeing its

aura. A mad hunt then began, and I found the auras of spiders, and ants, and flies. During the next days I then moved on to butterflies, birds, dogs, and cats. It was the same with them all. GOLD, pure GOLD, the energy of these, God's creatures, uncluttered, following their natural instincts, at one with nature and the pure order of the universe.

That was over fifteen years ago, and although it may not seem much to you as I recount it, to me it was a great discovery. Would I want to be a wood louse, my aura pure and beautiful? The answer: no, I like being who I am, a human being with clutter. But I could do with a little more GOLD in my aura, a little more purity in my heart, in my mind. I guess I'll just have to keep working at it. Maybe one day... with God's help...

Finally, the last but by no means least. The color *SILVER*. This color, in all its beauty, can be used to bring about the enhancement of spiritual love. What does that mean? Spiritual love? To understand, we have to remember the philosopher Pierre Teilhard de Chardin and his quote, which I use in my first book, *The Eagle and the Rose:* "We are not human beings having a spiritual experience; but spiritual beings having a human experience."

And Christ said, "Love thy neighbor as thyself." And we are all of God, even the woman who was rude to us as we shopped in the supermarket. Or the driver who screamed obscenities, or the man who practically knocked us over in his rush to catch the train. And so on. I think you know what I am trying to say. We all speak of tolerance, knowing we must strive to practice it. Knowing that sometimes we find it impossible. We speak too of love, of giving, of friendship. Yet we limit these things. To have spiritual love, to give spiritual love ... is to give someone a smile because you have it to give. Not because you want it returned. It is to put out your arms to someone and be unoffended if that person seems to turn his or her back on you. To do a good deed for the pure sake of it. Not requiring appreciation or acknowledgment ... simply giving from the heart, because you have it to give.

The color SILVER. This energy, fluid, liquid strands that move through the universe, silent, noiseless, and pure. This is the energy of purity.

In our world today, and especially in the Western world, we live each day with so much pressure. Pressure to succeed, pressure to achieve, pressure to survive. Many of us place ourselves deliberately under pressure. Pressure can be habit-forming. And pressure creates stress. The biggest killer in our society today. What exactly is stress? How can it be defined? According to Webster's dictionary, "Stress: a force that tends to distort a body—a factor that induces bodily or mental tension." A force that distorts, a force that brings about disharmony of mind, body, and spirit.

What, shall we ask, is healing? Healing is a force, an energy that restores, creates harmony, harmony of the spirit.

We all know about stress, and as a healer I would use a combination of soothing energy, color, to restore harmony.

But there is an emotion, more deadly, more damaging perhaps than any other. An emotion that can begin as a small seed, that can grow within the mind, distort the emotions, and seriously harm the soul.

As a child I grew up with this killer emotion. I watched as it destroyed my mother. It ate her up, consumed her, creating an angry and often spiteful human being.

Several years ago I felt this same emotion within me. My life was miserable; everything seemed to go wrong, no matter how hard I tried. Worse, I had to watch my child suffering. Overwhelmed, miserable, I felt something snap. I felt that same something, like a tiny, hard pebble, begin to rock, to move, deep inside, somewhere near my heart, my stomach, moving between the two, waiting to take hold.

Not caring, knowing this emotion for what it was, perhaps because as a child I had seen it in action so clearly, I waited, refusing to stop it, wondering if it would grow. Knowing, of course, that it could only take root and grow if I didn't stop it.

Days passed. The pebble rocked slowly backwards and forwards, it too waiting, waiting for the first signs of encouragement from me, so that it could take root. It needed a sign that it was welcome. I knew it was my decision. Aware of the invasion, almost, but not quite, welcoming it, not yet anyway, I reveled in self-pity and let it stay. It seemed the easiest thing to do. I was tired of fighting.

Then came the phone call. A young woman, her first words: "You probably don't remember me," she said. "I came to see you more than three years ago. My boyfriend was killed in an accident. You were able to make contact with him. My life was in ruins; I thought it was over. Bitterness was eating away at me. I was so angry with everyone, including him. You gave me a message from him, and this is why I am calling. You told me he said that if I destroyed my life, I would be destroying part of him too." Quietly I listened, wondering what it was that had made her call me now.

"I remember you told me, Rosemary, how, if we deliberately damage ourselves, how harmful it can be to our loved ones who have died. How our actions, good or bad, create reactions from them."

As she spoke these words, I felt Grey Eagle grow close. Knowing that for the last few days I had shut him out, I was grateful to have him there. "What can I do for you now?" I asked the young woman.

She replied simply, "Oh, I just wanted to say thank you. You have been on my mind today, and I wanted to let you know that my life now is good. I am happy and at peace with myself. I am not bitter anymore, and it's all due to you."

There was a click as the receiver went down, and I sat for a while staring at the telephone. I had heard the message loud and clear. So wrapped up in my own misery, I had failed to see that not only had I been close to destroying myself, I had also been close to seriously harming my guide. How could I have been so selfish, so self-involved, so blinded by self-pity? Easy. I am a human being, merely mortal, and at times, very, very weak.

Again I felt the small pebble, not rocking now but sitting inside, heavy as a large stone. Ashamed, devastated that I could have hurt Grey Eagle, I knew what I must do. Reaching out to him, reaching out into the universe, I found the energy that I needed. The purest, the most beautiful and cleansing. I drew it around me, breathed it in, wanting to be healed. And I felt the pebble as it turned to dust and then was no more. I felt the emotion, its name was BITTERNESS, and I felt it die.

BLUE . . . GREEN . . . RED . . . ROSE PINK . . . MAUVE . . . PURPLE . . . GOLD . . . SILVER.

These are the colors that I as a healer will use. This is the energy that is available to me. It is available to all of us, and all we have to do is reach out. Use it caringly, use it sparingly, and use it lovingly, always lovingly.

Before You Take
a Step into Healing

"It was never my intention to become a healer."

I take these words from my first book, *The Eagle and the Rose*, in the chapter "Rosemary the Healer." For one thing, after my own experiences with doctors, hospitals, and sickness, having had kidney problems in my early twenties, I really felt that I did not have what it takes to give healing in the way that I saw other healers do.

Other people's illnesses reminded me of my own vulnerability, my own weaknesses, and, of course, my own fear.

In the beginning the responsibilities of a healer were something I felt unable to deal with. But my spirit guide, Grey Eagle, was with me, and as my confidence grew, I learned gradually to accept my role as a healer.

These were my feelings all those years ago, when I took my first baby steps. Since then I have had many students who have, through time, learned the healing art. I too have been a student, learning, growing, gaining, and then sharing the knowledge I have. Some of that knowledge, a few small exercises, make up this book. However, absorbing the knowledge, perfecting the exercises, does not give you a "cure-all" ability, nor does it mean that you are now a full-fledged "healer," who has the ability to "heal" or "cure" others. The information contained in this book is designed to help you give love and healing to your soul . . . to give light to your spirit. As often happens, once the soul is at peace, then the physical body responds, and the physical healing takes place. But there are no guarantees that this will happen; no promises are made.

As you work on yourself, learn more, and become more enlightened, then of course you will be able to share with others that which you have learned. If you have a loved one, a relative or friend, who is sick and in need of healing, then you will be able to help. Sit with that person, hold that person's hand, and just as you have learned to do for yourself, now visualize your "patient." Follow the seven steps (see page 49), keeping in mind that person whom you are trying to help. As you pray, ask your higher power for help, guidance, and protection. Do not ask for what you feel is best for your patient, for to do that, you would be trying, unconsciously, to impose your will upon the will of heaven. This you cannot do. Rather, trust in your God, trust in the will of heaven, trust that God is the best judge of your patient's needs. How hard it can be for us to do this, especially when that someone we love is sick and dying and all we want is for him or her to live, to be given a cure. And there is always this one more thing that you can do: you can always ask for a miracle.

As a healer, seeing so much suffering, particularly with children, I have felt anger and despair. Have called out angrily to God, "How dare you do this ... how can you see such suffering and pain and do nothing?" And I have called out so many times, "Please, God, help them, help them, and please, God, help me."

The role of a healer is not an easy one, and the responsibility is great. I have learned that it is not for me to presume what is best for my patient. Only God sees the bigger picture; only His eyes and His heart know our needs. So I have learned, and now must stress to you, that if you wish to give what you have learned to others, give only without expectation, give only with hope, give only with love, for it is simply love, pure love, that will reach another's heart, another's soul. And in that giving, and in that receiving, true healing begins.

We are all, I believe, born with the gift to heal. A child falls and grazes its knee. As we scoop up the child, instinctively we place our hands on the sore.

Most often we use those soothing words "Let me rub it better." Each of us is gifted in this way, able to help ourselves and able to help others. What we cannot do, must not do, is interfere with God's will.

Recently I was asked to give healing to a small child, three and a half years old. This little girl was partially deaf, blind, and unable to breathe through her nose. She had had seizures and as a result suffered a weak heart. Her mother desperate and afraid, looking for a miracle, had written to me. Where was I to begin?

I leaned over the cot where the child lay. She looked the size of an eighteen-month-old baby. On her head was a headset, and her hands clutched a small cassette recorder, which she constantly switched on and off. Music was playing softly in her ears, but I could barely hear it. So then, where was I supposed to start? If I had not had all my years of training, I might have been terrified of the responsibility I was faced with. But I have learned that I am a spiritual being, even though my human state has its limitations. This was a time when, even knowing my own power, all I needed to be was a powerful yet clear channel for healing.

I sat next to the child, placing my hands on her gently, careful not to startle her. Bowing my head, I sent out a prayer, to God, to that great universal power, asking only, "Thy will be done." Five minutes passed, and I became aware of the most beautiful light. I watched, knowing, feeling the presence of God, and of angels. The light grew brighter, swirling around and around, encasing the child, protecting the child. Looking now to the mother, who was bending over her child, I reached out my hand and stroked her face.

"This child is a special child, a precious child," I whispered to her. "A child who has been given as a great gift to you. A child who will cause you such pain, so many tears, but yet a child who will teach you the true meaning of love, of joy, and of life."

I looked back to the child. Her hands had become still. Her eyes were closing. All through my body I could feel energy, healing energy flowing. Flowing into me, then out to my patient. I did not try to help, except now to place my hands upon the child's head. All I could be was a clear channel. God did the rest.

However, there are ways to help. Another time, perhaps with a patient who is suffering from a tumor, remembering that I own the power, that universal God-given power, even as I unite with God in the healing process, even as I am aware that God is in charge, that I must not interfere with His will, even so, I can combine my energy with His. The first thing I might do is to visualize the tumor. Reaching out into the universe, I will feel the varying levels of energy, each level a differing degree of vibration. Each different vibration seen as a color. Many vibrational levels, many colors. Visualizing the tumor, visualizing the colors, I would encase the tumor in light. Deep, penetrating light, a mixture of the colors I might chose to use. Then I might visualize the tumor shrinking, becoming smaller and smaller. Each time I gave healing to this patient, I would repeat the process.

So, even though we cannot dictate God's will, and even though there are those times when all we can hope to be is a clear channel, even so, there are ways to be really involved. Healing is an art, an art that takes time, patience, and dedication to perfect. Before taking these first steps, seven baby steps, to improving your health and well-being, allow me to share with you the words which I as a healer, will speak to God, words spoken in gratitude and all humility.

"I will do thy will."

Seven Steps Toward Self-Healing

Before we begin the process of healing, either for ourselves or for others, we need some guidelines. Here are seven simple steps, designed to be used as a guide toward our aim.

STEP 1

A. First we must ask ourselves these questions:
Why do I need healing?
What is my goal?

B. Keep a record. Make a note of any improvements in your condition or state of mind, no matter how small.

C. Decide from the start how often you want to do this exercise. Once a day? Once or twice a week? Then set aside that time. Make a note on your calendar, and stick to it as much as possible.

Be realistic about how much time you can give each week, but remember, each session needs to be no longer than ten to fifteen minutes. There is no maximum or minimum requirement, but the more often you do the exercises, the more you personally will get out of it.

STEP 2

A. Reread the color chart (see inside back cover).
   Remind yourself what each color signifies.
   Make a mental note of which colors feel right for you.

B. It is helpful to wear something that makes you feel good: a warm, soft color. Perhaps a scarf or sweater. Choose the color carefully to suit the mood you wish to create. Check your color chart.

This is something you can do every day whether or not you are giving healing to yourself.

C. Choose your music. Soft and gentle meditation music. This is the time you might choose to use my meditation tape *Give the Gift of Healing*.

D. Find your place, somewhere you will be sure to be undisturbed. A place that feels good to you. A quiet room with a soft bed to lie on or a comfortable chair to sit in.

E. Switch on your music.
   Breathe slowly and relax.

STEP 3

A. Now is the time to connect with your higher power, and with that universal healing energy. This can be done simply and easily through prayer.

B. Let your thoughts flow.
   Form words, phrases that you might like to speak to God, to Allah, to Buddha . . . to whomever you spiritually connect with.

C. This is a prayer which I might use.

*Dear God, through whom I believe all things are possible,
hear my prayer.*

*Be with me now as I ask for the power of healing to be
given to me.*

Unite with me.

Draw close to me.

Protect me.

Allow me to feel your love, to see your light,

That I might embrace it

That my soul will be healed

That I may receive the gift of healing.

STEP 4

A. Beginning with the color *BLUE*, choose your image.
SKY — BLANKET — FLOWER — OCEAN —
ETC.

B. Example. Visualize yourself floating in a warm
BLUE sea, the waves lapping gently over your
body. The sun warm on your face, the sky *BLUE*
and cloudless. Everywhere is peace.

C. Example. Visualize a field of cornflowers, the color of summer sky *BLUE*. There is a gentle breeze that blows softly, catching the flower stalks, making the *BLUE* flower heads sway slowly back and forth, creating a rippling affect. Take one careful step, then another into the field. Dance with the flowers. Feel the powder *BLUE* petals brush your cheeks as you move with them. The sun is warm. The field is all *BLUE*, a healing *BLUE*, and as you drink in the scene, you become relaxed and peaceful.

STEP 5

A. Begin to control your breathing.

Breathe in slowly, through your nose, out through your mouth.

In through your nose, out through your mouth.

B. Your breathing has become regulated, easy, and relaxed. Take deeper breaths. Using your stomach muscles, as you breathe in through your nose, allow your whole body to take in a breath. Breathe in through your nose; inhale deeply yet gently;

breathe in through your solar plexus at the same time.

Exhale slowly. Repeat.

C. Now as you perfect this technique, breathe in the atmosphere that you have created around you. Breathe in the *BLUE* of the cornflowers. The color of sky *BLUE*, as you float aimlessly, wonderfully in the ocean. Breathe in the warmth and the comfort of the *BLUE* blanket that you have wrapped around you. Indulge in the joy and the peace that you have created.

STEP 6

A. Remind yourself now of your needs. Look to the reason you need healing.

Are you suffering from depression?

Do you have a back problem?

Are you suffering from cancer?

Do you need relaxation?

Is it that you simply need to enhance your well-being?

This is the time to remember your goal.

B. Still with your chosen image of *BLUE*, and having read the color chart, slowly and carefully, a little at a time, add other colors to your picture.

C. Example. You may want to visualize the *GOLDen* sand of the seashore.

D. Example. Perhaps a little *PINK* in the sky where the *GOLD* of the sun touches the *BLUE*.

E. Don't be in a hurry to "paint" your picture, and don't be frustrated if you struggle with visualizing. It takes time and patience. Remember, it is only practice that makes perfect.

STEP 7

A. The music is playing.
   You are breathing naturally and easily.
   Your imagery is working.
   All around you is peace.

B. Absorb it.

C. Let yourself relax into it.

D. Allow your heart, your mind, your spirit, to flow with the river of energy that you have just created. That energy which is of you and which is of God.

E. Sink into that unity, that energy, which is the pure power of healing.

The Healer/
The Patient

I would like to close this book with a story that is very personal to me, because it involves two very special people, friends I was very close to, as you will see.

Two men it was a great privilege, not only to know, not only to work with, but also, to love.

This is my tribute to them.

Richard was there almost from the beginning. Having come to me for a consultation in which I made contact with his brother, who had died of cancer some years previously, Richard was curious. Who was this woman? What was this all about? These and many other questions were in his mind, and so he came to one of our healing centers shortly after it opened.

As is the rule of the Rosemary Altea Association of Healers (RAAH), Richard came to the center for several months, experiencing healing and learning what it is like to be a patient, before he applied for student status with our organization. He wanted to learn. He wanted to explore his own spiritual capabilities. And he wanted to help.

Having been for many years a dedicated worker with the Samaritans, a British national help line organization, and also an active member of a group for the disabled and severely handicapped, Richard was clearly a caregiver. Now, joining our organization, he became, over a period of many years, one of my most dedicated and loyal students. A true healer.

It is often much easier to find help for someone you love than for yourself. Easier to seek out a doctor, a surgeon, a healer, for someone else. This is how it was for Cliff. His wife, Sally, was recovering from an illness, and after reading about the RAAH, and having come to one of my lectures, he thought we might be able to help.

After a few weeks Sally was fine, and because of other commitments, she stopped coming to our center for healing. But Cliff continued to come, and over a period of several years he became more than a patient: he became a friend. He would have loved to become a student and a healer, but his work schedule did not allow him the time for classes and the total commitment all healers must have. However, each week he would arrive at the center, have his healing, then talk to other patients, help wherever he could, take over the desk for us if we were short-staffed. And he was always bright, looking on the positive side, concerned, and showing his concern for the other patients, as well as the healers. We all loved him, and he became part of the team.

I was on my way back to England from America in the spring of 1996 when I got the news, and I headed immediately for the hospital. They were doing tests, I was told, and it looked serious. Everyone, including me, suspected the worst. Cancer is a terrible disease, but it is not necessarily fatal. There are many types of cancer that are now curable. But the word strikes terror anyway.

As I entered the hospital, I was not alone. My friends and fellow healers, Joan and Pat, had come with me. Each of us had our own thoughts, our own prayers, and our own faith. But each of us knew that although healing can and does work miracles, sometimes the type of miracle we get is not the one we hope for.

When someone we love is sick, it is natural for friends and relatives to pray that the sickness be taken away. That the physical body be made whole again, that our loved one be "cured." But a healer will never pray in this way. We can ask for help for the physical body, but we never ask for a "physical cure," nor would we begin to suggest how best God should give His healing. Rather, we would ask that we can be used as a channel for that divine healing energy which comes from God. That in some small way we can be of help to do God's will.

This might be the time when we would reach out, try to connect with, that multivibrational energy, that energy which manifests as many different colors. Using visualization, we would ask that our patient be filled with light, with color, with power, that his or her soul might absorb the healing it is being given. Knowing that the soul makes its own choice, knowing too that God will already be aware what that choice is.

A healer knows that all we can do is to share what we have. We can visualize color shrinking a tumor, or freeing a patient's lungs. These things we can do. But we can never insist, or push, or demand that another should accept this gift. We can only hope. For we trust that God knows what is best for our patient, that He knows what is right. So we do what we can do, understanding that it is all we can do.

This is such a hard lesson for a healer, but we accept that we cannot interfere with God's will. Nor in our hearts would we truly wish to.

Joan and Pat and I knew these things.

So also did Richard. So also did Cliff.

Silently I traveled up in the elevator with Joan and Pat to the fourth floor, and as we entered the corridor, my friends turned to me, waiting for my instructions.

"Where do we go first?" asked Pat.

Joan, following quickly, said, "Just tell us what you want us to do."

I looked at my friends, knowing their sadness, sensing their nervousness, understanding that they were looking to me, needing me to be strong. I sighed, my heart heavy, and full of sadness too, I said, "First we will go to Richard, and then we will see Cliff."

My friend Richard was lying on top of the bedcovers, fully awake and alert. Just moments before he had been given the results of his tests. Terminal cancer. There was nothing anyone could do.

He looked up as I approached the bed, and tears sprang to his eyes at the sight of me. Only moments passed before I was on the bed, and he was in my arms, and as I rocked him like a baby, he murmured over and over in my ear, "I'm so glad you have come, so glad you are here."

Time passed. Only a few weeks, and I visited him almost every day, until it came time for me to return to America. As we said our good-byes, we both knew it would be the last time we would be together, both of us on the earth plane. But as Richard had said to me, "Even a healer is not exempt from pain or from illness, and no one is exempt from the greater plan. And after all"—he had smiled at me—"when God calls, we all must go."

Sally and Tim, Cliff's wife and son, were at his bedside when we arrived. His daughter, Heidi, arrived later. As I held him, he whispered, "I feel so much better now you're here. Thank God you came." Then, looking me straight in the eye, he said, "I'm going to fight, you know. I'm going to fight this thing." I smiled at him, knowing he meant it, knowing he would. And for many long weeks he struggled and fought, his family fighting with him. Eventually the cancer claimed him, as I knew it would, and I thought of how valiantly, how bravely he had battled. Never a complaint, never a grumble, even in his worst moments. "Better to have fought and lost," he would say, "than never to have fought at all."

Both Richard and Cliff had healing. Some would see the results and say, "Much good did it do!" But healing is for the mind, for the emotions, for the spiritual needs, as well as the physical needs.

Cliff played his audiotape *Give the Gift of Healing* throughout his illness, every day and sometimes twice a day. It helped calm and soothe him. It reminded him of the spiritual strength he gathered from all of his years coming to the healing center, from all that he had learned, and from his faith. He had the love and strength and support of his family, and I know that they, and he, would say that healing works.

Richard, who was the deputy chairman of the RAAH, had struggled not only with his illness but with the frustrations of a dying man with so much left to do on this earth. His hopes, his dreams and plans for our organization were great, and his vision was that we would grow. He desperately wanted to be an active part of that expansion.

In those last days that I spent with him, I would hold his hand and we would talk of the future. "I feel that I still have so much to give," he said to me one day. Then, shrugging his shoulders, a smile on his face, "I suppose," he continued, "that I'll just have to give it in a different way." He looked into my eyes, my friend and fellow healer, and then said, "I'll always be there when you need me, and I'll do my part in the organization, no matter what."

As I write, I feel them with me, the healer and the patient. Good men, good friends. I see Cliff smile, and hear him as he speaks the words he would say to me from his hospital bed . . . "Onward and forward . . . onward and forward." I smile, turn my head a little . . . hear Richard's voice, see his face, his eyes. Christmas is just three weeks away, and in his hand I see a small silver star, maybe for the Christmas tree. I listen now, knowing he has something to say to me, to say to all of us. "A miracle, a miracle," and I hear him laugh. "I am one of God's small miracles," I hear him say, as gently, and with much love, his fingers stroke my cheek.

A Final Word
from Grey Eagle

As we have journeyed through this small book, we have heard the wisdom of Grey Eagle, that wisdom which he gladly, joyfully shares with us all. It is fitting that he should close now. A Shaman. A Healer. A Teacher . . . I ask him this one last question . . . at least for now.

Question: Grey Eagle, what thought would you like to leave us with?

Answer: I would like to leave you with a miracle.
    I would like to leave you understanding miracles.

I would like to leave you understanding that miracles are at your fingertips.

I would like to leave you with the understanding that each day is a miracle ... and each small part of every day is a miracle.

I would like to leave you with the understanding that each smile given freely, and with no thought of a smile returned, is a miracle.

And I would like to leave you with the thought that God is a miracle ... and that the universe and all it embraces is a miracle.

And I would like to leave you with the thought that even the smallest piece of grit ... the tiniest speck of dust ... wherever in the universe it lies ... is a miracle of creation.

And I would like to leave you with the understanding that in "Owning the Power" ... in each man "Owning the Power," you own the ability to form your miracles ... to make your miracles ... to accept and to absorb your miracles.

And I would like to leave you with the thought that there is magic ... true magic.

Each one will know the magic that a child has ... that a child will bring.

That each of you is a child of God ...

A child of the universe ...

And the universe says that each of you is a magic thing.

So, take your magic ... hold on to your miracle ... and, dare to be.

And, the universe will cry out with joy ...

And then behold ... a miracle will be formed.

And, these words I will speak to you. And, these words come to you truly, and from my heart ... and, this is my way of sharing my heart with all of you who have sat at my fire and who have warmed their hands at my fire ... and have joined with us endeavoring to discover some truths ...

And, so then, this last thought I will share with you ...

The Apache believe ... accept ... that the butterfly is the symbol of eternal happiness and joy.

And, I will say to you truly, and indeed from my very heart ... this is my wish for you.

The Logo of
the Rosemary Altea
Association of Healers

Egg shape is symbolic of life.

1. The unbroken ring of gold represents the spirituality of our lives.

2. The tepee represents the home of Grey Eagle, Rosemary's spirit guide.

3. The skin of the tepee is green, the color of peace, which represents harmony with nature.

4. The background is bright blue, the universal healing color.

5. The rock is representative of God's strength and is the foundation on which the RAAH was built.

6. The initials are of Grey Eagle, whose teachings inspired our founder to form our healing association.

7. The initials are of our founder, Rosemary Altea.

All outlines in gold represent purity and harmony.

The logo was designed by a former healer member of the RAAH, Gerald Mould, who passed into the spirit world on December 25, 1996.

And There's More

As I have traveled around the world, lecturing, teaching, I am asked one question, over and over again by those of you who want to learn, want to grow— that question—"What can we do, what exercises, how should we live, in order that we can become more sensitive, more in tune with our higher self, with the spirit world, and with the universe?"

This book, the exercises in this book, well, this is just the beginning. Those seven basic steps toward giving the Gift of Healing will naturally take you to a higher level of sensitivity, the first steps to AT-TUNEMENT. Do these exercises regularly, over a period of months. Prepare yourself for more. More learning, more growing. YOU OWN THE POWER. Be ready to use it. To develop it.

Learning about energy, learning to use it, to build it, to give healing, is simply the first stage of your development. Some of you will be satisfied with that. Others will want more. In my next book, *You Own the Power!*, there are more exercises, more lessons, more learning, more insights. Our learning never stops. As your teacher, I will guide you, gently, slowly, to a place of light and enlightenment. Be patient, as I will be—this is the first lesson.

TO CONTACT
ROSEMARY ALTEA

If you are interested in learning more about Rosemary Altea and her work, you can write to her at the following address:

Rosemary Altea
P.O. Box 1151
Manchester, VT 05254

If you wish to be placed on Rosemary's mailing list, please indicate that in your letter. Also, please let us know which of the following topics you are interested in learning more about:

- Rosemary's healing organization, the RAAH
- Future books, audiotapes, and videotapes

Please make sure to clearly print your name, address, and fax number. For reply, please send $2, U.S. currency only, to cover the cost of postage and handling.

Rosemary is also the author of other books, including *Proud Spirit*™, available from Eagle Brook, an imprint of William Morrow. She also wrote *The Eagle and the Rose*, available from Warner Books in paperback and on audiotape.

For information about a signed, special limited edition of *Proud Spirit*™, ask your local bookseller or write to:

Joann Davis
Eagle Brook, an Imprint of
William Morrow and Company, Inc.
1350 Avenue of the Americas
New York, N.Y. 10019